SCOTTISH DIALECTS

A selection of words and anecdotes
from around Scotland

by
Kathryn Buchanan

BRADWELL
BOOKS

Published by Bradwell Books
9 Orgreave Close Sheffield S13 9NP
Email: books@bradwellbooks.co.uk

British Library Cataloguing in Publication Data:
a catalogue record for this book is available from the
British Library.

1st Edition

ISBN: 9781910551141

Print: Gomer Press, Llandysul, Ceredigion SA44 4JL
Design and artwork by: Andrew Caffrey
Photograph Credits: iStock, SCRAN & the author.
Cover; all iStock

Scotland was once part of North America before the land mass broke away and became attached to Europe. During the Ice Age Scotland was buried under two miles of ice and it was only after the ice melted, about 8,000 years ago, that the land was inhabited.

The Romans built forts and roads in the Lowlands and Highlands and called the inhabitants *Picti*, *'the painted ones'*. However, they were unable to conquer the Picts and built the Antonine Wall from the Forth to the Clyde in AD 142 to keep the Picts confined.

This was unsuccessful and the Romans withdrew from Scotland in AD 158 and retreated behind Hadrian's Wall, a more substantial structure built of stone in AD 122.

The Scots arrived from Ireland, Angles came from England and, in the 8th century, the Vikings invaded. Eventually, the Scots created the Christian Kingdom of Scotland that included everyone – except the Vikings.

Scotland now has a population of around five million with just over 20 per cent of its people living in Glasgow and Edinburgh. Aberdeen and Dundee are the next two largest cities by population, so this book concentrates on these four cities, the northerly islands of Orkney and Shetland, and the Western Isles. There are many parts of Scotland not included here and it has been a difficult task deciding what to leave out and what to put in. Hopefully, this little book will give you a flavour of Scotland and the diverse dialects that you may come across in a country where the total number of inhabitants is about 60 per cent of the population of London!

Fàilte gu Alba!
Kathryn Buchanan

Glossary

This little book explores a few of the dialects spoken in Scotland and the words are coded **Doric** *(D)*, **Dundee** *(Dun)*, **Glaswegian** *(G)*, **Orcadian** *(O)* and **Shetlandic** *(S)*. There are no codes after words that are in general use in Scotland. Some Gaelic words are included although this is a language and not a dialect.

A

Aberdeen – Aibirdeen *(Dun)*
Above – abeen *(D)*, abuin *(O)*, abune
Apple core – dump *(G)*, casket, stump

B

Bad-tempered – crabbit
Beach – ayre *(O) (S)*, traigh *(Gaelic)*
Beautiful – bonnie
Bed – scratcher *(G)*, böl *(S)*
Beetle – gablo *(O)*, hundiclock *(S)*, bittle
Be quiet – wheesht *(G)*, shoosh *(G)* hadd dee tongue *(S)*, had yir wheest *(O)*
Bin man – scaffie *(D)*, midgie-man *(G)*
Black eye – keeker

Bottom, backside – dowp *(D) (Dun)*, bahookie *(G)*,
rump *(O)*, erse *(O)*, *(Dun)*
Bounce – stoat
Boy – loon *(D)*, beuy *(O)*, laad *(S)*, laddie *(G)*, bitcallant *(D)*,
boay *(G)*
Bright – bricht *(D)*, lichty *(Dun)*
Brother – bridder *(S)*, sutshkin (sibling) *(S)*, brer *(Dun)*,
brither *(O) (G)*
Bucket – peel *(O)*, pail *(G)*
Bumblebee – foggy bummer *(D)*, drummie-bee *(S)*, droner
Butterfly – kailieflee *(O)*, butterie *(Dun)*

C

Chat, gossip – banter *(D)*, claik *(D)*, news *(S)*,
blether *(G) (O)*
Chatter, talk rubbish – bleeter *(D)*, bledder *(S)*,
blether *(O)*, yatter
Cheat – swick *(D) (S)*, chait *(Dun)*
Child, baby – bairn *(D) (O) (Dun)*, wean *(G)*, infant bairn
(S), ting *(S)*, peedie-breeks *(O)*, wee babby *(G)*
Chimney – lum *(G) (Dun) (O)*, shimley *(S)*
Church – kirk
Clean – dight *(O) (G)*
Cloud – clood *(D)*
Cold – caul *(D)*, Baltic *(G)*, atteri *(S)*, cawld *(O)*,

6

Bahltic *(Dun)*, cald *(Dun)*

Cough – hosst *(O)*, crim *(S)*, hauch

Cupboard (built-in) – press *(Dun) (G)*, aumrie *(O)*

Cup of tea – fly *(D)*, cuppa *(G)*

D

Dagger – biodag *(D)*, dirk

Dead – away a place *(G)*, deid *(O)*, deed

Devil – Mellishon *(S)*, Auld Nick *(O)* deil *(O)*, divil *(Dun)*, pelkie *(O)*, Auld Clootie *(G)*

Dirty – clarty *(D)*, clestered *(S)*, boggin *(G)*, manky *(Dun)*, eltit *(O)*

Dizzy, dazed – kringly-headed *(O)*, heidlght *(O)* in a dwam *(G)*

Dog – bratch (female) *(D)*, hund *(S)*, dug *(G)*, doag *(O)* *(Dun)*, bikko (female) *(O)*

Down – ben *(D)*, doon *(G) (S) (O)*

Drain – cundie *(Dun)*, stank *(G)*, Syer *(O)*

Drunk – bleezin' *(D)*, stocious *(D)*, paloovious *(S)*, mortal *(G)*, paralytic *(G)*, blootered *(O)*, steamin' *(G)*

E

Ears – lugs *(D) (S) (G) (Dun)*

Earwig – forkie-tail *(O)*, hornie-golach *(Dun)*

Edinburgh – Auld Reekie

Embarrassed – black affrontit *(D) (G)*, black affrontid *(O)*, minter (red-faced) *(Dun)*

Empty – teem *(D)*, töm *(S)*, tuim *(O)*

Entertaining, very good – teckle *(Dun)*

Every – ilka *(D)*

Exhausted – forfauchan *(D)*, trachied *(D)*, deeskit *(O)*, disjaskit *(S)*, wabbit *(G)*, laid by *(S)*

Eyes – een *(S)*

F

Fairy – trow *(S)*, hill-trow *(O)*

Farm – garth *(O)*, ferm *(O)*

Father – faider *(S)*, Da *(G)*, faether *(O)*

Ferry – aiseag *(Gaelic)*

Few – puckle *(D)*, twartree *(S)*, twa *(O)*

Fizzy drink – ginger *(G)*, skoosh *(G)*, scoot (lemonade) *(Dun)*

Foolish – doited *(D)*, fuilie *(O)*, glaiket *(G)*, tuim-heidit

Frown – glunch *(D)*, snurl *(S)*

Fuss – fams *(S)*, freck *(O)*, stramash, palaver

Children playing in
Ladywell, Livingston
on a Go-cart, Bogie
or Piler

West Lothian Archives
and Records Centre

G

Ghost – bogle *(D)*, bawkie *(O)*, wraith
Girl – quine *(D)*, tittie *(S)*, lassie *(G)*, lass *(O)*
Glaswegian – Weegie
Go – geng *(S)*, gae *(Dun)*, gae *(O)*
Go-cart – bogie *(G)*, piler *(Dun)*
Going – gyaun *(D)*, gawn *(G)*, gyung *(O)*
Good – braw *(G)*, rerr *(G)*, göd *(S)* guid *(O)*
Goodbye – mar sin leibh *(Gaelic)*, cheerio *(G)*
Grandfather – aald daa *(S)*, granda *(G)*, daa *(O)*
Grandmother – minnie *(S)*, nana *(G)*, grannie

H

Hailstones – haily-puckles *(S)*, hailstaines *(G)*, hailie-puckles *(O)*

Half-penny – bawbee *(D)*, hauf-penny *(G)*, maik *(Dun)*

Happy, pleased – blide *(O)*, chuffed *(G)*, canty *(S)*

Harbour – acarsaid *(Gaelic)*

Hare – bawd, bawtie

Heather – lyng *(O)*, hedder *(S)*

Hello – halò *(Gaelic)*, cheers *(G)*, aye, aye *(O)*

Hide (something) – plank *(G)*, hiddle *(S)*

Highland cattle – muckle coos

Home – bonhoga *(S)*, hame *(S) (G)*, heem *(O)*

Househusband – kettle-biler *(Dun)*

How – hoo *(Dun) (O)*, foo *(D) (S)*

Hug – bosie *(D)*

Hut – shiel

I

I – Ah *(G) (O)*, Ae *(Dun)*

Ice cream cone – pokey hat *(G)*

Idiot – föl *(S)*, edjit *(G)*, numpty *(G)*, feel gype *(D)*, bampot *(G)*, *(Dun)*, nyaff *(O)*

If – gin *(D)*

Incomer – eens fae aff *(O)*, ferry-looper *(O)*

In front of – fernent *(O)*

Jacket – coat *(O)*, jaiket *(G)*, jeckit *(Dun)*

Jam – jeely

Journey – stramp *(S)*, vaege *(S)*

Jumper – gansey *(O)*, jersey *(G)*, jerjy *(Dun)*

K

Knickers – draa'ers *(D)*, drawers *(G)*, drarz *(Dun)*, scants *(G)*

Knitting needles – wires *(S)*

Know-all – sclaterscrae *(S)*

Laughing, giggling – lauchin' *(D)*, gelderin' *(O)*, skirlin' *(S)*, cheeteran *(O)*

Lake – Loch (can be fresh water or sea water)

Lord or landowner – Laird

M

Man – min *(D) (Dun)*, Jimmy *(G)*, man-buddie *(O)*

Meal, food – bursten *(S)*, tea (dinner) *(G)*, scran *(G)*, maet *(O)*

Mess – sotter *(D)*, aggle *(O)*, clashnmelt *(S)*, murgadge *(S)*, midden *(G)*, plester *(O)*

Midge – mudjo *(O)*, mudjick *(S)*, midgie *(G)*, mijce *(Dun)*

Moan, whine, complain – weh *(O)*, maen *(S)*, girn *(G)*

Mole – mowdiewort

Money – penga *(S)*, cally dosh *(G)*

Mother – mither *(D) (O)*, midder *(S)*, mammy *(G)*, mithir *(Dun)*

Move house – flit *(D) (G) (O)*

Muddle – raffle *(O)*, fankle *(G)*

My – me *(S)*, ma

N

Nearby – near-haand *(S)*, near haun *(G)*

New Year's Day – Newerday *(S)*, Ne'erday *(G)*, Neuar-day *(O)*

Night – nicht

No – naw *(G)*, na *(O)*, nae

None – nane *(S) (G)*

Now – eenoo *(S)*, noo

O

Obey – answer *(O)*
Off – aff *(G) (S) (O)*
Old – auld
Old-fashioned – backaboot *(S)*, auld farrant *(O)*, auld fashioned
One – wan *(S) (G) (O)*, een *(S) (D)*, ane *(O)*, yin

P

Paper bag – poke *(G)*
Pencil – calafine *(S)*, pinsil *(Dun)*
Pillow – cod *(O)*, puhlae *(Dun)*, pilla *(G)*
Poison – pooshan *(D)*, pooshon *(O)*, pushion *(G)*
Porridge – gruel *(S)*, groal *(O)*, doing time in the Bar L *(G)*, Brose *(G)*
Potatoes (mashed) – shappit tatties *(S)*, bashed tatties *(G)*, chappid tatties *(O)*, champit tatties
Puffin – Tammy norie *(S) (O)*

Q

Quarrel, argument – töllie *(S)*, argie-bargie *(G)*, stramash *(Dun)*, stooshie
Question – whiss *(S)*, quaistion

R

Rabbit – moppie *(O)*, kyunnen *(S)*, bunny *(G)*

Rain (fine) – dagg *(O)*, driv *(O)*, drizzle *(G)*, raag *(S)*, smirr, muggrofu (rain with mist) *(O)*

Rain (heavy downpour) – rashan *(O)*, lashin' *(G)*, tömald *(S)*, stoatin' *(G)*, teemin' *(G)* vaanloop *(S)*, poorin *(Dun)*, ootfa *(O)*, peltin' *(G)*

Ready – clair *(S)*, duin

Remember – mind

Round – roon

Roundabout – circle *(Dun)*, roondaboot

Run – pin *(S) (O)*, styooch *(S)*

S

Salt cellar – saat-cuddie *(S)*

Sandwich – piece *(G)*, peece *(Dun)*

Seagull – whitemaa *(O)*, cullya *(O)*, skorie *(S)*

Scarf – gravit *(S) (O)*

Scold – flite *(S)*, flyte *(O)*

Scone – kröl *(S)* brönie *(S)*

School – skail *(D)*, schuil

Seal – sylkie *(S)*, selkie *(O)*

Shake – shugle

Sheep – yowe *(S)*

Shirt – sark *(D) (S) (O)*
Shopping – messages (groceries) *(G) (O)*, Errans *(O)*
Sister – sutshkin *(S)*, skin 'n' blister *(G)*
Sky – lift *(O) (S)*
Smack (hit) – skelp
Smash, break – pan *(Dun)*, tan *(G)*
Small – minkie *(S)*, mootie *(S)*, peerie *(S)*, toaty *(G)*, peedie *(O)*, sma, wee
Smell – gink *(G)*, waageng *(S)*, guff *(O)*, bowfin *(Dun)*, reek
Spinning – birling *(D) (G)*, whirlin', birlan *(O)*, birlin *(Dun)*
Speak – spik *(D)*, spaek *(O)*
Snow – sna *(D) (O)*, moor *(S)*, sneeb *(S)*, snaw *(G)*
Snowdrift – snowfang *(O)*, fann *(S)*
Snowstorm – blindroo *(O)*, mell-moorie *(S)*
Stay, staying – bide *(D) (O) (Dun)*, bade, stiy *(Dun)*
Smoke (fire) – rikk *(D)*, rook *(S)*, reek
Suspect – jalouse *(D) (S) (O)*, dreed *(S)*
Swollen, swelling – heuved *(O)*, hivvet *(S)*

T

Tell-tale – clashpie *(S)*, clipe *(D) (G) (O)*, clash-pie *(O)*
Thank you – cheers *(G)*, ta
Then – syne *(D)*, be dat *(S)*, than *(O)*
Thumb – toom *(S) (O)*
Tired – waabit *(D)*, ootdön *(S)*, wabbit *(G)*, puggled *(O)*

Tooth – yackle (molar) *(S) (O)*, teeth *(O)*
Trousers – breeks*(O) (S)*, jooks *(G)*, kegs *(G)*, brikks *(D)*, troozirz *(Dun)*, trews (tartan trousers)
Tummy, belly – puggy *(O)*, mogie *(S)*
Twilight – simmer dim *(S)*, gloamin' *(G)*, grimleens *(O)*
Two – twa

U, V

Ugly – ill-faared *(S)*, hackit *(Dun) (O) (G)*
Umbrella – gamp *(Dun)*, brolly *(G)*
Unexpected – oonlippened *(S)*
Uproar – deray *(D)*, hooro *(S)*, rookery *(O)*
Very – aafil *(S) (O)*, awfy *(G)*, gey
Vest – semmit *(D) (O)*, joopie *(S)*, simmet *(G)*, simmit *(Dun)*, singlet

W,X,Y Z

Waterfall – fors *(O)*, watterfa' *(G)*
Way – wye *(D) (G)*
Weep, cry – grat *(D)*, greet *(G) (O) (Dun)*, sprech *(S)*, bawl *(Dun)*
Well – weel
What – fit *(D)*, whit *(Dun) (G) (O)*
When – fan *(D)*, whan *(Dun)*

Where – far *(D)*, whaur *(Dun)*, whaar *(S)*, whar *(O)*

Whisky – screecham *(S)*, uisge-beatha *(Gaelic)*, John Barleycorn

White – fite *(D)*

Who – fa *(D)*, wha *(S)*, whar *(O)*

Whole – hale *(D) (S)*

Why – how *(G)*

Wicked – wanchancy *(D)*, ill-vicket *(S)*, weekid *(O)*

Witch – Rudas Carline *(D)*, Grotti Minnie *(O)*, Lucky Merran *(S)*

Women – wifies *(D)*, wiyfees *(Dun)*, wummen *(G)*, weeman *(O)*

Woodlouse – slatero *(O)*, sclater *(S)*, slater

Woolly hat with bobble – tourie *(D)*, toorie *(O)*

Work – wark *(D)*, wirk *(G) (O)*, ooril (work slowly) *(S)*

Yes – aye *(G) (O)*, yae *(S)*, ya *(O)*

You – du *(S)*, ya, yah, ye *(G)*, thoo *(O)*, yi *(Dun)*

F W Woolworth & Co premises, 119 Union Street Aberdeen, 1937
Aberdeen City Council, Arts & Recreation Department, Library & Information Services.

Aberdeen

The city of Aberdeen lies between the River Dee and
the River Don and traditionally it was reliant on fishing,
textiles, papermaking and shipbuilding. Since the discovery
of oil fields in the 1970s, it has become well known for its
flourishing offshore oil and gas industries. These industries
brought prosperity to the Granite City, so called because
granite was used for constructing the buildings, giving them
a sparkly look due to the high mica content. The Rubislaw
Quarry opened in 1740 and produced around six million
tonnes of granite before it closed in 1971. His Majesty's
Theatre, the Central Library and St Mark's neoclassical
church are all built in granite.

Doric dialect is spoken in the north-east of Scotland, particularly around Aberdeen. The Dorians of Ancient Greece lived in Sparta and were considered a bit uncivilised by the city dwellers of Athens, so the Doric dialect was considered 'rustic'. Doric was also used to describe the dialect of Lowland Scotland and Northumbria. Many of these Aberdonian words are also common in Newcastle upon Tyne, a port on the east coast, further south in England, where the dialect was also influenced by trade with Germany and Scandinavia.

Sea Beach with bathing huts, Aberdeen c. 1920
Aberdeen City Council, Arts & Recreation Department, Library & Information Services.

Div ye spik 'i Doric?

A'm awfu sair needin the lavvy – I need to go to the toilet now

A'm fair dancing mad – I'm really annoyed about this

Ay, Ay, fit like? – Hello, how are you?

Ay michty aye – Yes, that's right

Caumie doon! – Calm down!

Come an' hae a peek – Come and have a look

Come away ben the house – Come inside

Crombie – Cashmere coat

Dinna be coorse – Don't be naughty

Dinna fash yersel – Don't worry

Far dive ye bide? – Where do you live?

Fit like, mannie? Foos yir doos? - Hello, how are you? Keeping well? (The reply is (repetition important): *'Aye, peckin' awa! Aye peckin' awa!'* Meaning, I'm fine, thank you.)

Fit's adee? – What's wrong?

Furry boot ye frae? – Where do you come from?

Gie's a bosie! – Give us a hug!

Guidman's grund – An area of arable land left unplanted to appease the devil

Roustabout – A labourer on an oil rig

Shop till yer hairt's content – Shop till you drop!

The Bloo Toon – Peterhead

The Broch – Fraserburgh

Aberdeen Angus, shortbread and bawd bree

Prize-winning Aberdeen Angus istock

Around Aberdeen there is a great interest in food, and this area is famous for Aberdeen Angus beef, locally caught fish, Baxter's soup, and shortbread made by Dean's of Huntly where you can watch the process from their viewing gallery and visit their shop and Café Bistro. Walkers at Aberlour started producing shortbread in 1898 when JOSEPH WALKER opened his first bakery and it is still a family business.

Some local fayre:

Bawd bree – hare soup

Butteries – breakfast rolls (rawies) made with lashings of butter and lard

Cabbi claw – salt cod served with eggs, potatoes and parsley

Cappie wi' juicy – ice cream cone with raspberry sauce

Clabbie dubhs – mussels

Cullen skink – smoked fish soup (first made in a Buchan village, so it is said)

Finnan haddie – haddock smoked in Finnan

Hairy tatties – mashed potatoes with salt fish

Rumbledthumps – a mixture of potatoes and cabbage

Stappit heidies – stuffed fish heads

Aberdonians are said to be a wee bit tight-fisted and it may be that copper wire was invented by two Aberdonians fighting over a penny!

They also have a reputation for being a wee bit mean and so it is said that Aberdonians were amongst the first in Scotland to install double glazing so that their bairns couldn't hear the icer (ice cream van)!

The Buchan Vet *(traditional song)*

Oh, Ah come fae a wee toon in Buchan,
Far Ah practised for near forty year.
Ah'm the lad that's aye soucht when yer horse or yer nowt,
Are lookin' a wee bittie queer.
So if you see a stirk in the neuk o' a park,
Wi' his hair up and lugs hingin' doon,
Jus you get yer plooman tae jump on his bike,
And get the best vet in the toon!

Witches

JANET HORNE was the last witch burnt in Dornoch in 1727. In Scotland over 4,000 men and women were put to death for witchcraft in the 170 years before the Witchcraft Act was repealed in 1736. Only Germany executed more witches than Scotland. Many others died while in custody and when they were tortured and branded. Some witches were banished instead of being put to death. In Scotland, no evidence was needed and the law relied on 'habit and repute'. Tortures, punishment and burnings were paid for by seizure of property; or if they had no assets the local community or landlord had to fork out the cost. In Aberdeen in 1596, the cost of burning JANET WISHART and ISOBEL CROCKER was £7.9s Scots.

Bad luck for fishermen?

Fish processing factory Aberdeen, 1958 National Museums Scotland.

It seems that just about everything brings bad luck to fishermen and they certainly do not want ministers or women on their boats, or even to pass them on their way to work. One way to deal with some of these bad luck tokens was to give them other names, so rabbits were called fower-fitters or mappies, and pigs were sonnie cammies. Other actions were also feared, such as whistling against the direction of the wind, and if your jumper was on inside out it had to stay like that as changing it may be a bad omen.

The City of Dundee *(Gaelic: **Dùn Dèagh**)*

The city of Dundee is on the River Tay and built around an extinct volcano called The Law. Dundee's growth, prosperity and commercial success can be traced back to EARL DAVID *(1144–1219)*, the younger brother of WILLIAM I *(1143–1214)*, King of Scots, who was also known as *'The Lion'* not due only to his valour but also because of the red lion rampant on a yellow background that he adopted as his heraldic symbol. Under the direction of Earl David, Dundee developed into a prosperous trading port.

Royal Standard of Scotland, the Lion Rampant iStock

Raw wool was exported from Dundee in medieval times, followed in the 15th century by the production of finished textiles. In the mid-18th century the textile industry was revolutionised by the introduction of large four-storey mills as the 1742 Bounty Act granted subsidies for exporting Osnaburg linen, a plain coarse textile made from flax, tow or jute. However, the phasing out of the subsidy between 1825 and 1832 stimulated demand for cheaper and tougher textiles. At its peak, the textile industry boasted sixty-two mills employing 50,000 people. Scotland's Jute Museum @ Verdant Works gives an insight into the manufacturing process and the lives of the workers.

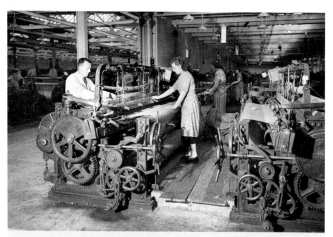

Jute Mills Dundee: Flat loom weaving in process
The Scotsman Publications Ltd.

RMS Discovery iStock

The rise of the textile industry benefited whaling as whale oil was required for jute manufacture. Dundee was a major whaling centre and robust ships were built here to withstand the inhospitable Arctic ice. With all this expertise available it is no surprise that Captain Scott's Antarctic research ship the RRS DISCOVERY was built here. She has now returned home to Dundee and this historic ship, which tells the story of polar expeditions and the men who served on her, is open to the public.

Dundee is the home of D.C. THOMSON, who have been publishing newspapers since 1886 and are famous of *the Sunday Post, The People's Friend, The Scots Magazine* and the *Beano* and *Dandy* comics and characters such as MAW BROON, OOR WULLIE and DESPERATE DAN, who now has his own app and features on YouTube.

Bonnie Dundee

During the Jacobite uprising, JOHN GRAHAM of Claverhouse, 1st Viscount Dundee, raised the Stuart standard on Dundee Law in support of JAMES VII (James II of England). SIR WALTER SCOTT wrote a poem in 1825 in his honour. Bonny was a common name for the town of Dundee and Scott called the Viscount 'Bonnie Dundee'. The original version has changed over time and here are a couple of verses:

To the Lairds o' Convention 'twas Claverhouse spoke,
'Ere the King's crown go down, there are crowns tae be broke;
Now let each Cavalier wha loves honour and me,
Come follow the bonnets o' Bonnie Dundee

Chorus:
Come fill up my cup, come fill up my can,
Come saddle my horses and call out my men,
And open the West Port and let us gan free,
And we'll follow the bonnets o' Bonnie Dundee!

Dundee he is mounted, he rides up the street,
The bells are rung backward, the drums they are beat;
But the Provost, douce man, said, 'Just e'en let him be,
The guid toon is weel rid o' that Deil of Dundee.'

Pehz, Pink Lint an' Peesez

Awa 'n' shuffle or **Aaw yi go!** – Away ye go!

Boabeez – Police

Cum awa fae there ye wee bison! – Come away from there you little devil!

Dookin' fir aipils – Bobbing for apples (Hallowe'en game)

Eezsel – Himself

Eh – I, yes, eye

Ehm – I am

Fairdeegowk – Frightened person

Fly-cup – Cup of tea and a biscuit in the afternoon

Gairden centir – Garden centre

Inginz – Onions

Loaby press – Cupboard in the hall

No affy weel – Not very well. *'Affy no weel'* is a more serious condition.

Peese – Sandwich

Peh – Pie

Pink lint – Cold meat

Saboot tyme – It's about time

Schnachters – Fancy cakes

Twa plen bridies an a inging ane ana – Two bridies without onions and one with onions

Whtna? – Do you want?

Whaur's mi baffies? – Where are my slippers?

Wid ye like a peese 'n' dip? – Would you like a slice of bread dipped in gravy?

Football

Dundee has two football clubs, **Dundee** and **Dundee United**. Their grounds are in the same street. When the local derby matches are played the players walk from their home ground to their away fixture.

Marmalade and Dundee Cake

It is said that JAMES KEILLER purchased a shipload of oranges from a vessel which sought shelter in the harbour and his wife, Janet, made a large quantity of marmalade with the oranges. From this beginning, Keiller built a business making quality marmalade. Keiller's also made traditional Dundee cake, a rich fruit cake made with dried and glazed fruit, decorated on the top with almonds.

Proverbs from the Kingdom of Fife

Fareweel, Bonny Scotland, Ah'm awa' tae Fife!
A deaf man will hear the clink o' money
Choose yer wife wi' her nightcap on

The Braes of Killiecrankie

The Pass of Killiecrankie is near Pitlochry and it was here on 27 July 1689 that the first shots in the Jacobite cause were fired. 'The Braes of Killiecrankie' commemorate this event and here are a couple of verses of this 18th-century song.

Whaur hae ye been sae braw, lad?
Whaur hae ye been sae brankie-o?
Whaur hae ye been sae braw, lad?
Cam' ye by Killiecranke-o?

Chorus:
An' ye had been whaur I hae been,
Ye wadna been sae cantie-o;
An' ye had seen what I hae seen
On the braes o' Killiecrankie-o.

I fought at land, I fought at sea,
At hame I fought my auntie-o,
But I met the deil and Dundee
On the braes o' Killiecrankie-o.

Orkney and Shetland Islands

Shetlandic is the dialect of the Shetland Isles and is said to come from the dialect brought to the islands by the lowland Scots from Fife and the Lothians, influenced by the Scandinavians. Old Norse, called Norn, used to be spoken in Orkney, Shetland and Caithness, but after Norway pledged these islands to the Scots in the 15th century the Norn language eventually became dormant. The Orcadian dialect spoken in Orkney still has remnants of Norse words and is considered soft and musical. Due to these islands' historic links with Norway, Gaelic is not spoken here.

Lerwick iStock

Orkney and Shetland are not two islands but archipelagos. Orkney has 67 islands with about 16 of them inhabited and they lie off the coast of Caithness. North Ronaldsay is the most northern island and Shetland is around 56 miles (90km) further north from here and it is about the same distance to Cape Farewell in Greenland. Shetland consists of over 100 islands with only 15 of them being inhabited. It is around a hundred miles (145 km) from Fair Isle to Out Stack, the most northerly point of Britain.

Orcadian Words and Phrases

Ring of Brodgar, Orkney iStock

Aak – Guillemot, nickname for people from Westray

Ah'm shurely fired hid oot – I must have thrown it out

Ah speered him – I asked him

Are you gittan? – Are you being attended to? (in a shop)

Assie pattle – A lazy person, nickname for a person from Sandwick

Back traet – Second evening of entertainment at an Orkney wedding

Beltane – An old Celtic fire festival when bonfires are lit on the hills

Best kens – Goodness knows

Blashy weather – Heavy sleety showers

Borrowween Day – 3 April, when you can borrow something and keep it!

Caa cannie – Take care

Cubbie Roo – A mythical giant who lived in Orkney

In a peedie while – In a few moments

Lice and nits jersey – A jumper knitted in parago which is a mixture of grey and white wool

Look ahint ye! – Look behind you!

Shaftin' his nave – Shaking his fist

Tae let be for let be – Call it quits

Wan coo, twa kye – One cow, two cows

Whit like the day? – How are you?

Whitna wey is yin tae dae hid? – Why are you doing it like that?

Skara Brae

Neolithic House, Skara Brae iStock

Few domestic structures from the Neolithic period survive anywhere in northern Europe and the discovery of this well-preserved village of eight clustered houses, older than Stonehenge, sometimes called the 'Scottish Pompeii', is quite extraordinary. In 1850 a violent storm devastated the Bay of Skaill, revealing the Neolithic remains which had lain buried since around 2500 BC, surviving undiscovered as the rapid advancement of sand-dunes effectively 'mothballed' the village. Amateur excavation took place but was abandoned in 1868 and it was 1924 before serious archaeological investigation began and work was undertaken to preserve the site.

The Neolithic builders used earth sheltering, that is sinking their houses into the ground, but in this instance they were sunk into pre-existing middens which would have provided a degree of insulation and warmth against the harsh climate. Although the visible remains give the impression of a well-ordered site, it is certain that an unknown number of additional structures have been lost due to sea erosion prior to the building of a seawall. Excavations suggest that the inhabitants were farmers, raising cattle and sheep, growing barley, eating eggs from seabirds like the Great Auk, shellfish and giant cod. The site was further from the sea than it is today and it is conceivable that a freshwater lagoon was nearby, protected by the dunes. Sometime around 2500 BC, the climate changed, becoming much colder and wetter, and the inhabitants may have abandoned the settlement. However, the precise reason is lost in time.

Scapa Flow

The name Scapa Flow derives from Old Norse, *Skalpaioi*, meaning *'bay of the long isthmus'*. It is an expanse of water in the Orkney Islands, about 30 metres (98 feet) deep, with a sandy bottom making it an immense natural anchorage of about 312 sq km or 120 sq miles. It was familiar to the Vikings, and KING HAAKON IV anchored his fleet here on 5 August 1263 at St Margaret's Hope. Scapa Flow is now better known as a naval base with associations to the German Navy. In response to the build-up of the German Fleet in 1904, the Admiralty became concerned that the Kaiser's fleet might slip into the Atlantic, threatening merchant shipping. Consequently, it was decided that Scapa Flow was ideal as a northern base, mainly because it offered a first-class anchorage, large enough to shelter the whole fleet. In May 1916, the fleet sailed from Scapa to engage the German Navy at the battle of Jutland on 31 May. This was the last time that two fleets engaged in a set-piece battle, Trafalgar style,

as in Nelson's day. At the armistice, 74 ships of the German fleet were interned in Gutter Sound at Scapa. After nine months waiting for the treaty to be agreed the German officer in command made the decision to scuttle the fleet to prevent the ships from falling into British hands.

Blockship sunk in Scapa Flow, Orkney Chick Chalmers

An Orcadian Riddle

Foweer hing-hangers,
An'foweer ching-changers,
An'een comes dinglan efter

An English version
Four hang, four walk,
Four stand skyward,
Two show the way to the fields
And one comes shaking behind

**The answer is a cow with its four teats, four legs,
two horns, two eyes, two ears and a tail.**

An Orkney Tongue Twister

This is from The Orkney Dictionary – recommended
reading and available from the Orcadian Bookshop.

Whither wid yi rather
Ur rather wid yi wjither
Hiv a stewed soo's snoot
Ur a soo's snoot stewed?

Shetlandic Phrases

Shetland Pony
iStock

Apon a stowen dunt – Without warning

Come awa in, wir blyde ta see you! – Come in, we're pleased to see you!

Da denner is ready – Dinner is ready

Da glesses is töm. What aboot anidder roond? – The glasses are empty. What about another round?

He göd ta da fishin back an fore – Now and again he goes fishing

He jöst lowsed – It's started to rain heavily

I'll awa am mak apo me – I'll away and get ready

Is du heard? – Have you heard?

No datn ill – Not so bad

True tale! – That's right!

Up Helly Aa

The Jaal Squad and the Galley Ship, 2015 iStock

Up Helly Aa, pronounced *'Up-he-lee-a'*, refers to any fire festival held in Shetland and derives from Old Norse meaning a holiday or festival, with the largest and most spectacular Up Helly Aa staged in Lerwck on the last Tuesday in January. The Lerwick celebration grew out of the older tradition of dragging burning tar barrels on sledges through the streets which took place on Christmas Day and New Year as well as Up Helly Aa. This potentially dangerous practice was abolished around 1874. The first Up Helly Aa torch procession took place in 1881 and the first replica Viking galley which is burned at the end of the procession was built in 1889.

The present-day festival comprises several hundred torch-bearers, all dressed in marvellous, eye-catching costumes, marching in procession behind a replica Viking galley through Lerwick. At the end of this spectacular procession, the marchers throw their torches into the galley and this is followed by a firework display. The celebration continues in various halls around the town late into the night.

The Shetland Bus

The Secret Intelligence Service established a base in Lerwick in the early stages of World War II. Initially, some of the crews of fishing boats coming back from Norway were asked if they would consider making a return trip taking agents out and bringing others back. This informal arrangement lasted throughout the winter of 1940–41 before becoming a more established group with the specific task of working for SIS and SOE, ferrying agents, weapons and radios to Norway. The German occupation of Norway commenced on 9 April 1941 and was completed by early May. Nevertheless, a number of Norwegians managed to escape, making landfall in Orkney and Shetland. The special operations group was set up by MAJOR LESLIE H. MITCHELL and LIEUTENANT DAVID HOWARTH RN, who ran the organisation from Flemington House, later renamed Kergord House, in Weisdale, with the boats operating from Lunna, north of Lerwick.

As well as running a regular, extremely dangerous 'bus service' ferrying agents and bringing out Norwegians who were under threat of arrest by the Germans, the group was involved with special operations, like the failed attack on the Tirpitz, a Bismarck-class battleship. The group made 198 trips to Norway and by the end of the German occupation the Shetland Bus had transported 192 agents, and brought 73 agents and 373 refugees out of Norway at a cost of 44 lives.

The Hebrides

The Western Isles are a chain of islands in the Atlantic Ocean off the north-west coast of Scotland, and are also known as the Outer Hebrides. Their Gaelic name is *Na h-Eileanan Siar* and 70 per cent of the population here speak Gaelic. This was the language of the Scottish law courts and royal courts which over the last 700 years has been replaced with English. The main islands are Lewis and Harris *(Leodhas agus na hearadh)*, Barra *(Barraigh)*, with Europe's only beach airport at Traigh Mhor, Benbecular *(Beinn nam Fadhla)* and South Uist *(Uibhist a Tuath)*.

The Inner Hebrides, *(Na h-Eileanan a-staigh)*, consist of 35 inhabited islands and over 40 uninhabited islands. The largest island is the Isle of Skye *(An t-Eilean Sgitheanach)* also known as the Island of the Mist *(Eilean a' Cheò)*. The other main islands are Ilsay *(Île)*, Jura *(Diùra)* and Mull *(Muile)*. Although there are fewer Gaelic speakers here than in the Outer Hebrides they are increasing and on Skye there is a Scottish Gaelic College, *Sabhal Mòr Ostaig*. Gaelic is a language and not a dialect, but as many signs are marked in both English and Gaelic and with its increased usage in this part of Scotland some words and phrases have been included here. If you would like to learn some basic Gaelic and how to pronounce it try the BBC Alba website at **www.bbc.co.uk/alba.**

Kisimul Castle, Castlebay, Isle of Barra, Outer Hebrides iStock

Gaelic phrases

Welcome – Fàilte

What is your name? – Dè an t-ainm a th' ort?

My name is … – Is mise …

How are you? – Ciamar a tha thu?

I'm well, thank you – Tha mi gu math, tapadh leat

Where are you? – Càite' bheil thu?

I don't understand – Chan eil mi 'tuigsinn

I am thirsty – Tha am pathadh orm

Cheers! – Slàinte!

Please – Ma's e ur toil e

Many thanks – Mòran taing

You're welcome – 'S e do bheatha

Good morning – Madainn mhath

Goodnight – Oidhche mhath

Goodbye – Slàn leat

Good luck! – Sealbh math dhuit/dhuibh!

Happy Birthday! – Là breith sona dhuit/dhuibh!

Merry Christmas! – Nollaig chridheil

Happy New Year! – Bliadhna nhath ùr

With best wishes – Le deagh dhùrachd

El mañana

There was a Spanish tourist on holiday on the Western Isles who used the phrase *'el mañana'* and one of the locals asked exactly what it meant. The Spaniard said that it meant sometime in the future, next day, next month, next year etc. The Scotsman replied, *'Ah, we dinnae hae a word in Gaelic for onything as urgent as that!'*

Gaelic Proverbs from *A collection of Gaelic proverbs and familiar phrases* by DONALD MACINTOSH, 1785

An ni nach cluinn thu 'n diu, cha 'n aithris thu maireach – What you do not hear today you will not repeat tomorrow

Bathadhmor aig oir thir – Wrecks are most frequent near the shore

Bi g'a curraigeach, brògach brochanach fa gheamhra – In winter be well hooded, well shod, and well fed with gruel

Buinigear buaigh le foidhidin – Victory is to be got by patience

Cha robh thu ftigh nar cha chiall a roinn – You were not at home when wisdom was dealt out

Harris Tweed *or* Clo Mor *(The Big Cloth)*

Hebridean woman stirring a vat during the dyeing of wool
in North Uist, 1940 National Museums Scotland.

LADY CATHERINE, Countess of Dunmore *(1814–86)* inherited
the Isle of Harris when her husband died in 1845. Here
she found the islanders starving and destitute and she
sought funds to help them immediately but also planned
for their long-term survival by encouraging home working
in knitting and weaving. She introduced Harris Tweed to
her society friends and promoted it through contacts in
Edinburgh and London.

Harris Tweed can only be made in the Outer Hebrides and must be **'Handwoven by the islanders in their homes in the Outer Hebrides, finished in the Outer Hebrides, and made from pure virgin wool dyed and spun in the Outer Hebrides'** *(Harris Tweed Act, 1993)*. However, some of the processes are now mechanised and the wool no longer comes exclusively from sheep bred on the islands of Harris and Lewis. Although there are still Blackface sheep here, as they are resilient to the harsh weather on the moors, wool from Scottish cross-breads and Cheviot sheep is also used today. This extends the range of Harris Tweed as these other breeds of sheep have softer, thicker fleeces and so softer, thinner fabrics can be woven.

The woollen mills on the islands deliver beams and bobbins of yarn to the weavers in their homes along with instructions and colourways from the designers in the mill. As the fabric is handmade, each weaver's tweed is different. The fabric is then returned to the mill, where any impurities are removed by washing in soda and soapy water, and then it is dried, steamed, pressed and cropped. When the material is flawless, the famous Harris Tweed trademark is ironed on to the fabric. Some weavers work for themselves and not the mill, designing their own Harris Tweed, and have their own retail customers who are looking for exclusive designs.

The Road to the Isles *(traditional song)*

Highland Cattle with the Cuillins in the background iStock

The far Cuillins are pullin' me away,
As take I wi' my crummack to the road,
The far Cuillins are putting love on me,
As step I wi' the sunlight for my load.

Sure by Tummel and Lock Rannoch and Lochaber I will go.
By heather tracks wi' heaven in their wiles.
If it's thinkin' in your inner heart, the braggart's in my step,
You've never smelt the tangle o' the Isles.

A tale of whisky which grew into a legend

The popular Ealing Studios comedy, *Whisky Galore!* starring BASIL RADFORD, BRUCE SETON, JOAN GREENWOOD and GORDON JACKSON was made in 1949 and is based on a novel of the same name by COMPTON MACKENZIE *(1883-1972)*, a prolific writer, who produced almost one hundred books. Both film and novel are based on the 1941 shipwreck of the SS POLITICIAN near the island of Eriskay and the unauthorised removal of the ship's cargo of 24,000 bottles of whisky by the islanders.

Briefly, in the film the inhabitants of an isolated Scottish island, Todday in the Outer Hebrides, have been unaffected by wartime rationing until whisky supplies run out in 1943. At this point gloom descends until suddenly events take a turn for the better when the freighter SS Cabinet Minister runs aground in thick fog. Two islanders row out to investigate and are euphoric to learn from the departing crew that the ship's cargo is comprised of 50,000 cases of whisky. A battle of wits ensues between the islanders who want to 'liberate' the whisky and the authorities who want to salvage the cargo.

In reality however, there was a twist to this tale. Official files released by the Public Records Office disclose that a substantial sum of cash in the form of eight cases containing nearly 290,000 ten-shilling notes was also part of the cargo being carried by the SS Politician when it ran aground. In April 1941, there were reports of banknotes, traceable to the wreck, turning up in Benbecula and in May an empty cash case was found in the ship's hold. By June notes were turning up in Liverpool and by 1943 they were found in London, eventually spreading as far afield as Switzerland and America. A total of 211,267 notes were recovered by the salvage company, a further 2,329 were presented at various banks but 76,404 have never been found!

Mair aboot whisky

Lagavulin Distillery Islay iStock

Whisky has been distilled in Scotland for over 500 years, probably originally being made by friars with rudimentary equipment. At first it was used for medicinal purposes to treat colic, smallpox and palsy and to preserve and prolong life. During the cold winters it was offered to travellers on arrival and as its popularity increased. Taxing whisky in the 17th century led to many a skirmish between the illicit distillers and the excisemen. At first whisky was made only from malt, but later also from grain and today many whiskies are blends of the two.

A Toast

Here's tae us:
wha's like us?
Gey few, and they're
a' deid.
Mair's the pity!

'Here's tae us'
iStock

Scottish comedian CHIC MURRAY *(1919–85)*, from Greenock, gave good advice about whisky, saying that there are two rules. Never take whisky without water and never take water without whisky!

> *'Eh, Angus, Whit is the new incomer like then?'*
> *'Ah went tae hiv a wee bit talk wi' him th'ither evenin' an' he offered me a glass o' whisky, d'ye see? Weel, he wis poorin' it oot an' Ah said tae him tae stop – an' he stoppit.'*
> *'Sae, that's the sort of man he is!'*

Iona *(Gaelic: Ì Chaluim Chille)*

Iona is a small island, 3 miles north to south and 1½ miles east to west. It was given to SAINT COLUMBA *(c.521–97)* by the local king soon after he came to Scotland in AD 563. Columba, with thirteen followers, founded a monastery as a centre for learning and artistic achievement and it became renowned for sending out missionaries to Scotland and northern England.

In 1203, the monastic order was reorganised under the Benedictine rule. The Abbey is the most elaborate and best preserved ecclesiastical building surviving from the Middle Ages in the Western Isles.

Westering Home *(Scottish folk song)*

Chorus:
Westering Home and a song in the air,
Light in the eye, and it's goodbye to care,
Laughter o' love, and a welcoming there,
Isle of my heart, my own one.

Tell me o' lands of the Orient gay,
Speak o' the riches and joys o' Cathay,
Eh, but it's grand to be walkin' ilk day
To find yourself nearer to Isla.

Chorus:
Where are the folk like the folk o' the west?
Canty and couthy and kindly the best;
There I would hie me and there I would rest
At hame wi' my ain folk in Isla.

Oban *(Gaelic: An t-Òban)*

Oban, meaning *'the little bay'* in Gaelic, is a Victorian resort town, known as the *'Gateway to the Isles'*. It enjoyed increased prosperity from the 1880s with the arrival of the railway. SIR WALTER SCOTT paid a visit in 1814 and the publication of his poem, *The Lord of The Isles*, the following year, brought many new visitors to the town. During World War II, Oban was an important naval base used by the Royal and Merchant Navies, assuming a new importance during the Cold War period because the first transatlantic telephone cable, carrying the famous 'hotline', came ashore at Gallanach Bay.

Oban, with its busy ferry terminal operating services to the Hebridean islands, has been dependent on tourism since the 1950s. Oban distillery has produced whisky since 1794 and is easily identified by its tall chimney. This distillery is one of Scotland's oldest producers of single malt Scotch whisky and for those who would like to know more there are guided tours and an interesting museum. The town's landmark, McCaig's Tower, built in imitation of Rome's Coliseum, stands on a hill, a stiff ten-minute walk from the quayside.

The town, due to its particular location, experiences cool summers and mild winters with temperatures rarely falling below zero due to the warming effect of the Gulf Stream.

Aurora Borealis

Aurora, from the Latin word *aurora* meaning sunrise or the Roman goddess of dawn and *borealis*, the Greek name for north wind, is a natural light display predominantly visible in the high-altitude regions of the Arctic and Antarctic. Aurora are caused by charged particles, mainly electrons and protons emanating from the sun, travelling towards the poles, drawn by the Earth's magnetic field and entering the atmosphere from above. This process causes ionisation and excitation of atmospheric gases, giving an exciting multi-coloured glowing light show. In the northern hemisphere they are known as the aurora borealis, hanging above Earth in an oval-shaped halo. The strength of auroral activity tends to run in eleven-year cycles. There is, of course, a southern counterpart known as aurora australis.

The best place to see the Northern Lights in Britain is in Scotland with the Caithness coast, the Orkney Islands and the Outer Hebrides popular spots because of low light pollution. Cold, clear autumn and winter nights are prime times for viewing.

Roon aboot Glesga *(Gaelic: **Glaschu**)*

Glasgow and the Clyde

It is said that Glesga made the Clyde and the Clyde made Glesga. By dredging and opening up this river, which flows from the Leadhills to the sea, Glasgow became an important port. In the 1900s it was known as the 'Second City of the Empire' as shipbuilding and trade brought wealth to the city.

In the 1700s, Glasgow was in the fortunate position of having a faster trade route than London to the lucrative tobacco fields of Virginia in America. Sailing from Glasgow was much faster, gaining forty days on a return trip.

The Tobacco Merchant's House The Author

The Glasgow Tobacco Lords took full advantage of this to increase the number of journeys made by their ships, making them exceedingly rich. There are streets named after them, including Dunlop Street and Ingram Street, and you can see a tobacco merchant's house at 42 Miller Street.

Glenlee Tallship outside the Riverside Museum, Glasgow iStock

Many ships were built in the yards on the Clyde and the workers were very proud of their achievements. The liners QUEEN MARY, QUEEN ELIZABETH and QUEEN ELIZABETH II were all built at John Brown's shipyard at Clydebank. The Riverside Museum on the banks of the Clyde is an interesting and child-friendly place and tells the story of shipbuilding, trade, commerce and transport. Designed by ZAHA HADID, the building is an awesome sight, on what used to be Inglis Shipyard on the north bank of the Clyde where it merges with the River Kelvin.

Roamin' in the gloamin'

A popular, romantic view of the River Clyde by SIR HARRY LAUDER

> *Roamin' in the gloamin' on the bonny banks o' Clyde,*
> *Roamin' in the gloamin' with a lassie by my side,*
> *When the sun has gone to rest,*
> *That's the time that I like best,*
> *Oh, it's lovely roamin' in the gloamin'.*

Glesga Patter

Ah'm urnae gonnae hurt ye! – I'm not going to hurt you (*'so long as ye do wit Ah tell ye'* …)

Are ye right? – Are you ready?

C'moan on, get aff! – This is where you get off the bus

Eh, no? – Isn't that right?

Fish supper – Fish and chips. Chippies also sell pie suppers, haggis suppers etc.

Geeza slug o' yer ginger – Give me a drink from your

bottle of lemonade

Gie it laldie, 'Ye cannae shuv yer grannie aff a bus…'
– Sing lustily, *'You cannot push your granny off the bus…'*

Glesga kiss – Head-butt

Gonnae geeza a haun? – Please help me

Gonnae no dae that – Don't do that

How's it gaun? – How are you?

Jammy piece – Jam sandwich

Jings, Ma, that dug's hoachin'! – Heavens above,
Mother, that dog has lots of fleas!

**Ma heid's loupin' so it is. How's that? Ah dinna
ken but mibbe a wee whisky 'ill sort it oot** – I have a
headache. Why is that? I don't know but perhaps a small
whisky is the answer.

Nae bother at aw – No problem

Shoot the craw! – Make a quick exit

The Subway or **Clockwork Orange** – Glasgow's
Underground Railway System

They've gan doon the watter fur the Fair – They have
gone to a seaside resort by sailing down the Clyde from
the Broomielaw for the Fair Fortnight (when the factories
used to close for two weeks in July)

Ya beauty! or **Ya dancer!** – Fantastic!

Ye ken fine well that … – Don't deny it, you know that…

Jimmy was blootered and he wis trying tae cross wan o' the big, wide streets in the toon. Ev'ry time he stepped oot intae the traffic he wis nearly hit by a motor. He tried quite a few times but got nae further than a few steps aff the pavement when he had tae stagger back tae save himsel' frae being knocked doon.

A helpful chap from Edinburgh came by and said, 'Do you know that there's a zebra crossing just up the road? Jimmy replied, 'Well, Ah hope he's hivin' better luck than me, pal!'

I Belong to Glasgow

This song was written by BILL FYFFE *(1885–1947)*, a Scottish music hall artist who was not from Glasgow but from Dundee. He observed an inebriated inhabitant of the city in the Central Station and asked him if he belonged to Glasgow and got the reply that *'at the moment, Glasgow belongs to me!'* and this inspired him to write this song. When Fyffe died a tragic death by falling from a hotel room window in St Andrews, he was buried in Glasgow.

I belong to Glasgow,
Dear ol' Glasgow toon;
But what's the matter wi' Glasgow,
For it's goin' roon an' roon

I'm only a common old working chap,
As anyone here can see,
But when I get a couple o' drinks on a Saturday
Glasgow belongs to me!

Fitba'

There is a passion for football in Glasgow, which is not surprising as the first international football match was held here in 1872.

Loch Lomond

Balmaha Village, Loch Lomond iStock

61

Loch Lomond is a freshwater loch lying on the Highland Boundary Fault and has the largest surface area of any inland water in Great Britain. It is part of the Loch Lomond and the Trossachs National Park and has more than thirty islands, some of them maybe crannogs, artificial islands built in prehistoric times. On the eastern shore, Ben Lomond rises to a magnificent 3,195 ft (974 m). The loch was formed during the Ice Age and amongst the great variety of fish here is the powan, a type of freshwater herring.

Only twenty miles from Glasgow, it is a popular destination for a wee hurl in the motor or to take part in a variety of water sports including canoeing, sailing, water skiing and wind surfing.

The Bonnie Banks o' Loch Lomond
(18th-century song)

On yon bonnie banks an' by yon bonnie braes
Whaur the sun shines bright on Loch Lomond
Whaur me an' my true love will ne'er meet again
On the bonnie, bonnie banks o' Loch Lomon'

Oh, ye'll tak' the high road, and Ah'll tak' the low road,
And Ah'll be in Scotland afore ye:
Fir me and my true love will never meet again
On the bonnie, bonnie, banks o' Loch Lomon'.

New Lanark Cotton Mills

New Lanark
Girls around
1920
New Lanark Trust

New Lanark cotton mills, situated to take advantage of the only waterfalls on the River Clyde, were planned and developed in 1785 by DAVID DALE *(1739–1806)*, a Glaswegian merchant banker and philanthropist, and RICHARD ARKWRIGHT *(1732–92)*, who in the 1780s was energetically promoting his water frame in Scotland and the continent. Four mills were constructed and water to drive the massive wheels was diverted from the Clyde by aqueduct and tunnel. As part of the mill complex Dale created a model industrial community, an example of utopian socialism, with a planned village and social facilities for the workers and their families.

New Lanark Pipe Band 1948 New Lanark Trust

The local population were reluctant to work long hours in a building outwardly resembling a workhouse, and there was also a general lack of enthusiasm for employment in 'manufactories', as these barrack-like buildings were known. To alleviate the shortage of workers, large families were recruited from other parts of Scotland with the whole family working in the mills, along with orphans and those who could be enticed by the prospect of work and housing.

By the early 1790s, New Lanark had a densely packed population of around 2,000 with half comprising teenagers and children and most of them working in the mills.

Social pioneer and mill manager, ROBERT OWEN *(1771–1817)*, who married David Dale's daughter Caroline in 1799, improved the conditions and provided free millworkers' houses, health care and education for the workers and the first workplace nursery school in the world. New Lanark is now a World Heritage Site and a visitor attraction where you can find out about the New Lanark cotton mills and village life.

Edinburgh *(Gaelic: Èideann)*
Scotland's Capital City

The City of Edinburgh is divided into two toons, the Auld Toon and the New Georgian Toon that is over 200 years old, so not really so new!

The Auld Toon has narrow passageways called closes, and stairs, lots of them. It was this overcrowded, smelly and smoky town that earned Edinburgh the name Auld Reekie. The Royal Mile runs from the iconic Edinburgh Castle, past St Giles Cathedral to Holyrood Palace and the Scottish Parliament. This is a toon steeped in history and atmosphere, and maybe even a few ghosts. It is said that on a quiet, calm day the skirling of bagpipes can be heard coming from under the Royal Mile as the ghost of a lost piper walks the secret tunnels that used to lead from the Castle to the Palace of Holyrood House where MARY, QUEEN OF SCOTS lived between 1561 and 1567.

You can still walk along the medieval underground passageways that were Mary King's Close, which was blocked off with the plague victims still inside to prevent the disease spreading. The Real Mary King's Close is a tourist attraction and you can see for yourself what Edinburgh was like in the 17th century before they built new buildings on top of the old. The old South Bridge Vaults are said to be haunted, and perhaps BURKE & HARE may have hunted for victims and stored their murdered bodies here while waiting to take them to the nearby University where they were in demand for dissection by Professor ROBERT KNOX. You can book a visit to the Vaults through Mercat Tours in Blair Street.

Just over the George IV Bridge is the Elephant House tea and coffee shop, a favourite haunt of authors such as J.K. ROWLING and ALEXANDER MCCALL SMITH, and along from there is the statue of GREYFRIARS BOBBY. This wee dog has a shiny nose as passers-by rub it in sympathy for his story of dedication to his master, as Bobby stayed by his grave until his own death.

The New Toon, in contrast, has wider streets, more imposing houses and delightful squares. Princes Street is renowned for its gardens and shops and behind here is George Street with St Andrew's Square, now a noisy public garden, at one end, and peaceful Charlotte Square at the other. To see what these houses were like when they were built, visit the Georgian House (National Trust for Scotland) at number 7 Charlotte Square. If you are a fan of Ian Rankin's detective, Rebus, the Oxford Bar is just round the corner from here in Young Street. Not far from here are the private Queen Street Gardens, and at Inverleith the Royal Botanic Garden welcomes everyone and entrance is free.

Charlotte Square The Author

Scottish words and phrases

Ah'm up to high doh – I am very anxious and at the end of my tether

A pint and a hauf – a pint of beer and a glass of whisky (chaser)

Auld Reekie – Edinburgh

Awa' an' bile yer heid! – Get lost, I have no time for you! (Literally: *'Away and boil your head'*)

In the name of the wee man! – Goodness me!

It's a sair fecht – It's a hard life

Lang may yer lum reek - I wish you prosperity and a long life (literally: *'Long may your chimney smoke'*)

Scotch – Only use this when referring to whisky, eggs, and mist – never people

Wee dram – A glass of whisky

Ye'll get yer heid in yer hauns to play with – You'll be in serious trouble (Literally: *'You will get your head in your hands to play with'*)

Bagpipes

'Did ye no hear aboot the piper that lived up a close in the New Toon?'
'Naw, Ah dinnae ken aboot that.'
'The neighbours complained aboot the racket so he took aff his shoes!'

Coontin'

Jock wis jist back frae his first ever trip to France.

> 'Hoo did ye git oan wi' the lingo, Jock?'
>
> 'Och, Ah picked up a few wee words like oof fur egg and Ah fund oot that if ye jist say oof ye git wan egg.'
>
> 'Whit did ye dae if ye wanted twa eggs.'
>
> Ye say 'twa oofs' and they bring ye three eggs an' ye jist leave wan on yer plate!'

Tartan

For a time in Scotland it was bad news to wear tartan unless you were in the army. The penalties laid down in KING GEORGE II's Dress Act of 1746 included deportation for seven years! SIR WALTER SCOTT invited KING GEORGE IV to visit Scotland in 1822, and for this special occasion Scott declared 'let every man wear his tartan'. Many clans hurried to have a special tartan made just for their family, and by the end of the 19th century just about every clan had its own tartan. There are many shops in Scotland where you can buy kilts, tartan gifts and clothing, but do not worry if your family does not have its own tartan as there is now a choice of universal tartans such as the Hunting Stuart, Flower of Scotland and Pride of Scotland.

Ah expect ye'll hav hid yer tea?

Weegies have been known to say that this is a traditional welcome from Edinburgh folk, who hope you have had a meal before you turn up at their door, tea being an evening meal and not a cuppa!

Scottish Cuisine

Burns Night is the 25th January and traditionally the supper starts with cock-a-leekie soup followed by haggis, neeps and tatties, and then Scotch trifle or cranachan.

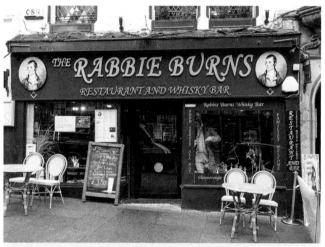

Rabbie Burns Restaurant and Bar on the Royal Mile, Edinburgh iStock

Haggis, neeps, tatties and a wee dram The Author

Hogmany is New Year's Eve and a time for some stodgy food before the drinking begins in earnest, so try a good helping of steak pie and tatties.

Bannocks – these are oatcakes cooked on a griddle

Bridies – are pasty shaped and contain meat and sometimes onions. They vary throughout Scotland and a baker in Forfar claims to have invented them in the 1800s. In this area short crust pastry is used but mostly they are made with flaky pastry.

Cock-a-leekie soup – chicken and leek soup; traditionally includes prunes

Clapshot – mashed potatoes and turnip

Cranachan or **Cream Crowdie** – raspberries, oatmeal, a wee dram, cream or cottage cheese or crème fraiche

Edinburgh Rock – comes in sticks which are coloured, very sweet with a rough texture but melt in the mouth

Haggis – a mixture of oatmeal and offal, original cooked in a lamb's stomach but now also available in tins

Hot toddy – whisky, lemon, honey and hot water – a comforting drink when under the weather

Irn-Bru – a carbonated soft drink, *'made in Scotland from girders'* and is extremely popular

Kedgeree – smoked haddock, rice and curry powder, served for breakfast

Lorne sausage – this comes either square sliced or round but is not like bangers (these are called links). They are named after comedian Tommy Lorne *(1890–35)*, who grew up in Glasgow and made many jokes about square sliced and used the catchphrase *'Sausages is the boys!'*

Pokey hat – ice cream cone

Porridge – porridge oats traditionally cooked in water with salt sprinkled on the top, but now often made with milk and topped with honey

Scotch pancakes – flat, round and cooked on a griddle

Scotch pies – pastry filled with mutton – often sold at hauf-time at the fitba'

Shortbread – sweet and buttery type of biscuit

Stovies – potatoes, onions and leftover meat cooked together in gravy

Sybies – spring onions

Tattie Scones – usually triangular shaped and made from mashed potatoes and cooked on a griddle or a flat pan

Port of Leith

Fisherrow fishwives knitting East Lothian Library Service.

It was common for women to knit during their breaks from work or while waiting for the herring boats to arrive and even while walking and carrying peat on their backs. This is multi-tasking in a big way as the patterns were often complicated and intricate. Fair Isle patterns are distinguished by two colours of wool in each row and make lovely warm jumpers. Shetland lace knitting, with its delicate lace-type patterns, is so fine that it is said that a shawl can be pulled through a wedding ring.

Leith lies north of Edinburgh city at the mouth of the Water of Leith. On 19 August 1561, MARY, QUEEN OF SCOTS, aged

18, landed here on her return from France, having sailed from Calais because QUEEN ELIZABETH I had denied her passage through England. She arrived at Leith (even then one of the largest European ports) earlier than expected and, finding no welcoming party, she was taken to dine in the finest house in Leith, owned by a prominent merchant and landowner, ANDREW LAMB.

Leith was formerly a port with trading links to members of the Hanseatic League, a traditional alliance which exercised extensive moral, diplomatic and economic power, having 200 member towns at its height. Founded in the 13th century, it survived until the 17th century.

After World War II, the dock area suffered serious decline. In the 1990s Leith docks benefited from large-scale investment and regeneration, claiming to be the largest waterfront development in Europe. Now it is the most extensive deep-water port in Scotland and an important berth for ships operated by the northern European cruise industry, handling some sixty cruise ships and 30,000 passengers every year.

Ocean Terminal is Edinburgh's largest shopping and leisure complex and where the ROYAL YACHT BRITANNIA is berthed. She was built by John Brown & Co. at Clydebank and launched on 16 April 1953, at a cost of over two million pounds, and is now a visitor attraction. The ship carries a Rolls Royce Phantom V, complete with on-board garage.

Some traditional industries of the past include the **Leith Glassworks** on Bolton Street, dating from 1746. In 1770, peak production was one million wine bottles per week, largely exported to France and Spain. Around then the company started to manufacture crystal glass mainly for chandeliers, under the name of Edinburgh Crystal Company. Sanderson's distillery was based in Leith from 1863, famous for VAT 69 and Mountain Dew Scotch blends, and moved to South Queensferry in 1969.

Rose's Lime Juice was founded by Lachlan Rose on Commercial Street in 1868 to provide Vitamin C in the form of juice to prevent scurvy. From early in the 19th century, sailors in the British Navy were required to take a measure of lime juice with their daily ration of rum.

Noo, here's some faur-kent folk

JOHN LOGIE BAIRD *(1888–1946)*, born in Helensburgh, was an engineer and he sent the first television picture a few feet across a room in 1924. He made his apparatus from old bits of cardboard, string, a tea chest, a washstand, sealing wax and a biscuit tin.

SUSAN BOYLE *(born 1961)*, a singer from Blackburn in West Lothian, rose to fame after appearing on television's Britain's Got Talent in 2009.

SCOTT BRASH *(born 1985)* is a showjumper and was born in Peebles. As part of the British Team he won a gold medal at the London 2012 Olympics.

ANDREW CARNEGIE *(1837–1919)* was born in Dunfermline in Fife in a cottage which is now a museum dedicated to him. He emigrated to America, where he made his fortune, and endowed the first of over two thousand free public libraries in Dunfermline in 1863. His philanthropic works included the Carnegie Trust for the Universities of Scotland.

JIM CLARK *(1936–68)* was a racing driver who won two Formula 1 World Championships in 1963 and 1965, and twenty-five Grand Prix races. Born in Kilmany in Fife, his family moved to Duns and he went to school in Chirnside and Edinburgh. There is a museum dedicated to him in Duns.

SIR ARTHUR CONAN DOYLE *(1859–1930)* was born in Edinburgh and is famous for his Sherlock Holmes novels.

DAME EVELYN GLENNIE *(born 1965)* was born in Aberdeenshire and is a world-renowned percussionist who has won many musical awards and received honorary doctorates. Her success is even more remarkable as she has been profoundly deaf since the age of 12.

KENNETH GRAHAME *(1859–1932)*, author of *The Wind in the Willows*, was born at number 30 Castle Street in Edinburgh's New Town.

JAMES KEIR HARDIE *(1836–1915)* was from Lanarkshire and later his family moved to Govan in Glasgow. He started work at seven years old as a messenger boy for a steamship company and at ten years of age he went to work in the mines. He became a Member of Parliament and was a founding member of the Labour Party.

DR DAVID LIVINGSTONE *(1813–73)* was born in Blantyre in South Lanarkshire. At the age of 10 he started work in the local cotton mill. In 1838, he became a student at the Charing Cross Hospital Medical School and then went to Africa as a medical missionary and explorer.

CHARLES RENNIE MACKINTOSH *(1868–1928)*, an architect and artist, was born is Glasgow. His designs included the Glasgow School of Art, the Willow Tearooms for Miss

Cranston, and the Hill House in Helensburgh.

CATRIONA MATTHEW *(born 1969)* is a world-famous golfer from North Berwick in East Lothian. From being Scottish Girls Champion in 1986 she has gone on to win four LPGA tours and six European tours.

ANDY MURRAY *(born 1987)*, the tennis player, was born in Glasgow. He won Wimbledon in 2013 and was voted BBC Sports Personality of the Year. At the London 2012 Olympics, he won gold in the men's singles and silver in the mixed doubles.

CHRIS PATERSON *(born 1978)*, rugby player and coach, was born in Edinburgh and went to school in Galashiels. He is Scotland's record cap and points holder.

SAMUEL JOHN PEPLOE *(1871–1935)*, a Scottish post-impressionist painter, was born in Edinburgh and one of the group called the Scottish Colourists along with JOHN DUNCAN FERGUSSON, FRANCIS CADELL and LESLIE HUNTER. Paintings by Peploe may be seen in the National Galleries of Scotland in Edinburgh.

IAN RANKIN *(born 1960)* was born in the Kingdom of Fife and his crime novels, especially those with Edinburgh-based detective Rebus, have achieved international popularity and are quite addictive. Ian Rankin's Edinburgh is available as an app **(visit www.ianrankin.net)**. Rankin has won four Crime Writers' Association Dagger awards and been presented with an OBE for services to literature.

J.K. ROWLING *(born 1961)* wrote parts of her *Harry Potter* novels at various locations in Edinburgh, including the Elephant House and Black Medicine Coffee Company cafés.

SIR WALTER SCOTT *(1771–1832)*, born in Edinburgh, became a lawyer, poet and writer. Edinburgh's railway station, Waverley, was named after one of his novels and there is an enormous monument to him in Princes Street Gardens.

MARY SLESSOR *(1848-1915)* was born in Aberdeen and later her family moved to Dundee. She went to West Africa as a missionary and set up schools, hospitals and churches and successfully campaigned to end the killing of widows.

JAMES WATT *(1736–1819)* from Greenock improved the stream engine that had been used to power water and windmills so that it could power locomotives, ships and factory machinery.

Bibliography

BAILEY, P, (2007) *Orkney*, Devon: David and Charles.

BUCHANAN, K. (2014) *Eclectica Glasgow*, Sheffield: Bradwell Books.

DALHOUSIE, F. (2014) *Eclectica Edinburgh*, Sheffield: Bradwell Books.

FLAWS, M. and LAMB, G. (2005) *The Orkney Dictionary*, Orkney: The Orkney Language and Culture Group.

HOLLAND, J. (2008) *Exploring the Islands of Scotland: The Ultimate Practical Guide*, London: Frances Lincoln.

O'DAY, J.P. (2014) *The Illustrated Dundee Dictionary*, lulu.com.

SANDERSON, K. (2014) *Glaswegian Dialect*, Sheffield: Bradwell Books.

www.harristweed.org

Acknowledgements

Thank you to everyone who shared their favourite words, food, songs and places with me. A special thank you to ALASDAIR SINCLAIR and JOHN SANDERSON for their ideas, contributions and assistance.

Photograph credits: those not credited individually © KATHRYN BUCHANAN